HUSTLE

A GUIDE TO
SOCIAL MEDIA
MARKETING

TABLE OF CONTENTS

By following these beginner-friendly steps, you can gradually build a presence on social media that attracts an audience and generates income over time.

Choose Your Platform

Choosing the right social media platform is crucial when aiming to make money through social media. Each platform has its own unique audience demographics, content formats, and monetization opportunities. Here's a detailed exploration on how to select the best social media platform for monetization purposes:

Understanding Platform Demographics and Audience

Firstly, consider the demographics and user base of each platform:

- **Instagram**: Known for its visual content, Instagram attracts a younger audience, particularly those under 35 years old. It's ideal for industries like fashion, beauty, lifestyle, and travel due to its highly visual nature.

- **YouTube**: A video-centric platform, YouTube appeals to a broad demographic, including younger audiences and adults. It's suitable for content creators who can produce high-quality video content, tutorials, product reviews, and entertainment.

- **TikTok**: Growing rapidly among younger demographics, TikTok is known for short, engaging videos. It's great for viral content, challenges, and quick product demonstrations, making it suitable for brands targeting Gen Z and millennials.

- **LinkedIn**: Geared towards professionals and businesses, LinkedIn is ideal for B2B marketing, networking, and showcasing expertise through articles, posts, and video content.

- **Facebook**: With a wide-ranging user base across different age groups, Facebook is versatile for various types of content including text, images, and video. It's effective for building communities, running ads, and selling products directly through Facebook Marketplace.

Evaluating Content Types and Formats

Next, consider the types of content that perform well on each platform:

- **Visual Content**: Platforms like Instagram, Pinterest, and TikTok thrive on visually appealing content such as photos, graphics, and short videos. These are effective for showcasing products and lifestyle content.

- **Video Content**: YouTube, Facebook, and TikTok are excellent for video-based content, including tutorials, product reviews, vlogs, and entertainment. Video content tends to have higher engagement rates and can facilitate affiliate marketing and ad revenue.

- **Written Content**: LinkedIn and Twitter are suited for text-based content such as articles, posts, and tweets. These platforms are effective for sharing industry insights, thought leadership, and engaging in professional discussions.

Monetization Opportunities

Consider the monetization options available on each platform:

- **Advertising Revenue**: Platforms like YouTube and Facebook offer ad revenue sharing programs based on views and engagement with ads displayed on your content.

- **Sponsored Content**: Influencers on Instagram, TikTok, and YouTube can collaborate with brands for sponsored posts, product placements, or endorsements, earning fees based on their reach and engagement rates.

- **Affiliate Marketing**: Suitable across various platforms, affiliate marketing involves promoting products or services and earning a commission on sales generated through your referral links. Platforms like Instagram and YouTube are particularly effective for showcasing products and driving affiliate sales.

- **Selling Products or Services**: Platforms like Instagram (through Instagram Shopping), Facebook Marketplace, and YouTube (through video descriptions and links) allow direct selling of products or services to your audience.

- **Subscription and Paid Content**: Platforms like Patreon (for exclusive content) and LinkedIn (for premium subscriptions) offer opportunities to monetize through subscriptions or gated content.

Analyzing Your Target Audience and Goals

Lastly, align your platform choice with your target audience and business goals:

- **Audience Reach**: Choose platforms where your target audience is most active and engaged. Consider their demographics, behaviors, and preferences when selecting the platform(s) to focus on.

- **Business Goals**: Define your monetization goals (e.g., increasing brand awareness, driving sales, building a subscriber base). Select platforms that align with these goals and offer the necessary tools and features to achieve them.

Section Conclusion

Choosing the right social media platform for making money involves a combination of understanding platform demographics, evaluating content types and formats, exploring monetization opportunities, and aligning with your target audience and business objectives. By strategically selecting and leveraging platforms that best suit your niche, content style, and goals, you can effectively monetize your social media presence and achieve sustainable income streams over time.

Define Your Niche and Audience

Choosing a niche audience is a critical step in leveraging social media to make money effectively. A well-defined niche allows you to tailor your content, products, and services to meet specific audience needs, thereby increasing engagement, loyalty, and ultimately, revenue. Here's a detailed exploration on how to choose a niche audience for making money with social media:

Understanding the Importance of Niche Audience

1. **Targeted Engagement**: A niche audience consists of individuals who share common interests, demographics, or behaviors. Targeting a niche allows you to create content that resonates deeply with your audience, leading to higher engagement and interaction rates.

2. **Market Differentiation**: Focusing on a specific niche helps you differentiate yourself from competitors. You can establish authority and credibility within your niche, becoming a go-to resource for your audience's specific needs.

3. **Monetization Opportunities**: Niche audiences often have specific purchasing behaviors and preferences. By understanding their pain points and desires, you can create products, services, or content that cater directly to them, increasing your chances of monetization through various channels like affiliate marketing, sponsored content, or direct sales.

4.

Steps to Choose a Niche Audience

1. **Identify Your Passions and Expertise**:

   ○ Start by identifying topics, industries, or hobbies that genuinely interest you and where you have knowledge or expertise. Passion for your niche will fuel your motivation and commitment to creating valuable content and offerings.

2. **Research Audience Demand and Trends**:

   ○ Conduct market research to identify potential niche audiences. Use tools like Google Trends, social media analytics, and keyword research to understand the popularity and demand for different topics within your chosen niche.

3. **Define Audience Demographics and Psychographics**:

○ Determine the demographics (age, gender, location, income level) and psychographics (interests, values, lifestyle) of your target audience. This information will help you tailor your content and marketing strategies to effectively reach and resonate with them.

4. **Evaluate Competition and Gaps**:

○ Analyze competitors within your chosen niche. Identify gaps or underserved areas where you can provide unique value or differentiation. Consider how you can offer something different or better to attract and retain your audience.

5. **Validate Audience Interest**:

○ Test your niche audience's interest and engagement potential through social media platforms. Start by creating and sharing content related to your niche to gauge audience response, feedback, and interaction levels.

6. **Refine Your Niche Audience Definition**:

○ Continuously refine your niche audience definition based on insights gathered from audience feedback, engagement metrics, and market trends. Adapt your content and offerings to better meet the evolving needs and preferences of your audience.

Examples of Profitable Niche Audiences

- **Health and Fitness**: Targeting individuals interested in fitness routines, nutrition tips, and wellness products.

- **Personal Finance**: Focusing on budgeting advice, investment strategies, and financial literacy for specific demographics (e.g., millennials, retirees).

- **Travel**: Catering to travelers interested in destination guides, travel hacks, and adventure experiences.

- **Fashion and Beauty**: Creating content around fashion trends, makeup tutorials, skincare routines, and product reviews.

- **Technology and Gadgets**: Providing tech enthusiasts with reviews, comparisons, and updates on the latest gadgets and innovations.

Implementing Monetization Strategies

Once you've chosen your niche audience, consider various monetization strategies:

- **Affiliate Marketing**: Promoting products or services relevant to your niche and earning a commission on sales generated through your referral links.

- **Sponsored Content**: Collaborating with brands to create sponsored posts, reviews, or endorsements that resonate with your audience.

- **Digital Products**: Creating and selling digital products such as e-books, online courses, templates, or exclusive content tailored to your niche audience.

- **Membership or Subscription Services**: Offering premium content, community access, or exclusive perks through membership or subscription models.

Section Conclusion

Choosing a niche audience involves identifying a specific group of individuals with shared interests and needs, understanding their demographics and behaviors, and offering tailored solutions or content that provide value. By focusing on a niche audience that aligns with your passions and expertise, you can effectively leverage social media platforms to build a loyal following, drive engagement, and generate sustainable income streams over time.

Create Compelling Profiles

Creating compelling profiles and accounts on social media is essential for making money as it helps you attract and engage with your target audience effectively. A well-crafted profile not only showcases your brand or persona but also establishes credibility, builds trust, and encourages interaction. Here's a detailed guide on how to create compelling profiles and accounts for monetizing your presence on social media:

1. Choose a Consistent Brand Identity

- **Profile Picture**: Select a clear and recognizable profile picture that reflects your brand or persona. Use a high-resolution image that is visually appealing and aligns with the tone of your content.

- **Username**: Choose a username that is easy to remember and relevant to your niche. Ideally, it should be consistent across all social media platforms to maintain brand coherence.

- **Bio**: Write a concise and compelling bio that clearly describes who you are, what you do, and what value you provide to your audience. Use keywords relevant to your niche and include a call-to-action (e.g., link to your website or latest product).

2. Optimize Your Profile for Search and Discovery

- **Keywords**: Incorporate relevant keywords in your bio and profile description to improve searchability. Use terms that your target audience might use when searching for content related to your niche.

- **Hashtags**: Use industry-specific hashtags in your bio and posts to increase visibility and attract followers interested in your niche. Research popular and trending hashtags relevant to your content.

3. Create High-Quality Content

- **Visual Content**: Use high-quality images, videos, and graphics that resonate with your audience. Visual content is crucial on platforms like Instagram, Pinterest, and TikTok for engaging your followers.

- **Consistency**: Maintain a consistent posting schedule to keep your audience engaged and interested. Experiment with different content formats (e.g., stories, reels, live videos) to keep your profile dynamic and engaging.

4. Engage with Your Audience

- **Respond to Comments**: Actively engage with your followers by responding to comments, questions, and messages promptly. This shows that you value their input and encourages further interaction.

- **Encourage Interaction**: Pose questions, run polls, or create interactive content that encourages likes, shares, and comments. This boosts engagement metrics and increases your visibility on social media algorithms.

- **Build Community**: Foster a sense of community among your followers by creating discussions, sharing user-generated content, and acknowledging loyal supporters. This strengthens brand loyalty and encourages word-of-mouth referrals.

5. Highlight Social Proof and Achievements

- **Testimonials and Reviews**: Showcase testimonials, reviews, or endorsements from satisfied customers, clients, or collaborators. This social proof enhances your credibility and trustworthiness.

- **Achievements**: Highlight milestones, awards, or notable achievements relevant to your niche. This reinforces your expertise and establishes you as a leader in your field.

6. Use Analytics to Refine Your Strategy

- **Monitor Performance**: Use analytics tools provided by social media platforms to track metrics such as follower growth, engagement rates, and content performance. Analyze which types of content resonate best with your audience and adjust your strategy accordingly.

- **Optimize Content**: Based on analytics insights, refine your content strategy by focusing on topics, formats, and posting times that generate the highest engagement and conversion rates.

7. Collaborate and Network

- **Partnerships**: Collaborate with other influencers, brands, or content creators within your niche to reach new audiences and expand your network.

- **Networking**: Attend industry events, join online communities, and engage in networking opportunities to build relationships and establish connections within your niche.

8. Stay Authentic and Transparent

- **Authenticity**: Be genuine and transparent in your interactions and content. Authenticity builds trust with your audience and enhances your credibility as a social media influencer or entrepreneur.

- **Disclosure**: Clearly disclose any sponsored content, partnerships, or affiliate links to maintain transparency and comply with social media guidelines and regulations.

Section Conclusion

Creating compelling profiles and accounts on social media involves strategically crafting your brand identity, optimizing for search and discovery, creating high-quality content, engaging with your audience, highlighting social proof, using analytics to refine your strategy, collaborating and networking, and maintaining authenticity and transparency. By implementing these strategies effectively, you can attract a loyal following, build meaningful relationships, and ultimately monetize your social media presence to achieve sustainable income and business growth.

Start Creating Content

Creating compelling content and mastering graphics are crucial skills for monetizing your presence on social media. High-quality visuals not only attract attention but also enhance engagement and convey professionalism. Whether you're promoting products, sharing expertise, or building a personal brand, here are tips and tricks for creating effective content and graphics to make money on social media:

1. Understand Your Audience and Goals

- **Audience Research**: Identify the demographics, interests, and preferences of your target audience. Understand what type of content resonates best with them and align your content strategy accordingly.

- **Goals**: Define your objectives for creating content (e.g., increasing brand awareness, driving sales, generating leads). Tailor your content and graphics to support these goals effectively.

2. Create Valuable and Relevant Content

- **Educational Content**: Share informative content such as tutorials, guides, tips, and industry insights. Position yourself as a knowledgeable resource within your niche.

- **Entertaining Content**: Create entertaining and engaging content such as memes, quizzes, challenges, or behind-the-scenes glimpses. Use humor or storytelling to captivate your audience.

- **Inspiring Content**: Share motivational quotes, success stories, or personal anecdotes that resonate with your audience's aspirations and values.

3. Tips for Creating Graphics

- **Use Consistent Branding**: Develop a cohesive visual identity with consistent colors, fonts, and design elements across your graphics. This builds brand recognition and reinforces your brand message.

- **Choose the Right Tools**: Utilize graphic design tools such as Canva, Adobe Spark, or Photoshop for creating professional-looking graphics. These platforms offer templates, stock images, and editing features to simplify the design process.

- **Eye-catching Thumbnails**: For platforms like YouTube and blog posts, create compelling thumbnails that capture attention and entice viewers to click. Include relevant text, high-quality images, and vibrant colors.

- **Infographics**: Present complex information or data in a visually appealing and easy-to-understand format with infographics. Use charts, icons, and concise text to convey key points effectively.

- **Typography**: Pay attention to typography by choosing readable fonts that complement your brand style. Experiment with font sizes, weights, and styles to create hierarchy and visual interest.

4. Optimize for Each Platform

- **Size and Format**: Tailor your graphics to fit the specifications of each social media platform. For example, Instagram posts may require square or vertical formats, while Facebook covers need specific dimensions.

- **Mobile Optimization**: Design graphics that are optimized for mobile devices, considering how they will appear on smaller screens. Ensure readability and visual appeal on both desktop and mobile platforms.

5. Engage Your Audience

- **Call-to-Action (CTA)**: Include clear CTAs in your graphics to prompt your audience to take action, such as visiting your website, subscribing to your channel, or making a purchase.

- **Interactive Elements**: Incorporate interactive elements like polls, quizzes, or clickable links within your graphics to encourage engagement and interaction.

6. Monitor Performance and Iterate

- **Analytics**: Use analytics tools provided by social media platforms to track the performance of your content and graphics. Monitor metrics such as engagement rates, click-through rates, and conversions.

- **A/B Testing**: Experiment with different graphic styles, colors, and messaging through A/B testing. Determine which variations resonate best with your audience and optimize accordingly.

7. Stay Updated with Trends

- **Visual Trends**: Stay informed about current design trends and adapt your graphics to reflect popular styles. Incorporate trending colors, patterns, and visual motifs to stay relevant and appealing to your audience.

8. Compliance and Ethics

- **Copyright**: Respect copyright laws when using images, fonts, or design elements in your graphics. Use royalty-free images or purchase licenses for stock photos to avoid legal issues.

- **Disclosure**: If your content includes sponsored posts, endorsements, or affiliate links, disclose these relationships transparently to maintain trust with your audience and comply with advertising guidelines.

~ Content Bonus Section ~

Social Media Creatives

Creatives refer to the visual elements and design choices that bring your content to life, making it more engaging, memorable, and effective in achieving your monetization goals. Here's how to effectively utilize creatives to make money on social media:

1. Understanding the Role of Creatives

- **Visual Appeal**: Creatives encompass the overall aesthetic and visual appeal of your content, including graphics, images, videos, and animations. They play a key role in capturing attention and conveying your brand's message effectively.

- **Brand Identity**: Creatives help establish and reinforce your brand identity across social media platforms. Consistent use of colors, fonts, logos, and design elements in your creatives enhances brand recognition and builds trust with your audience.

2. Types of Creatives for Social Media

- **Graphics**: Create eye-catching graphics such as promotional banners, product images, quote cards, and infographic-style posts. Use tools like Canva or

Adobe Spark to design visually appealing graphics quickly and easily.

- **Images**: Utilize high-quality photos and visuals that align with your brand and resonate with your audience. Consider using professional photography or stock images to enhance the visual appeal of your posts.

- **Videos**: Incorporate video content into your social media strategy, including tutorials, product demonstrations, behind-the-scenes footage, or engaging storytelling. Videos tend to attract higher engagement and can effectively convey your message.

- **Animations and GIFs**: Add movement and interactivity to your creatives with animations or GIFs. These dynamic visuals can capture attention and communicate messages in a concise and engaging manner.

3. Tips for Effective Creatives

- **Clear Messaging**: Ensure your creatives communicate your message clearly and effectively. Use concise text, impactful visuals, and a strong call-to-action (CTA) to guide your audience towards the desired action.

- **Visual Hierarchy**: Arrange elements within your creatives to create a clear visual hierarchy. Highlight important information or CTAs using larger fonts, contrasting colors, or strategic placement within the design.

- **Branding Elements**: Incorporate consistent branding elements such as logos, color schemes, and fonts into your creatives. This reinforces your brand identity and ensures continuity across all your social media posts.

- **Emotional Appeal**: Appeal to emotions through your creatives by using imagery and colors that evoke specific feelings or responses from your audience. Emotionally resonant creatives tend to foster deeper connections and engagement.

4. Testing and Optimization

- **A/B Testing**: Experiment with different creative styles, formats, and messaging through A/B testing. Measure the performance of each variation to identify what resonates best with your audience and optimize future creatives accordingly.

- **Performance Analytics**: Use analytics tools provided by social media platforms to track the performance of your creatives. Monitor metrics such as engagement rates, click-through rates, and conversion rates to gauge effectiveness and make data-driven decisions.

5. Staying Creative and Innovative

- **Stay Updated**: Keep abreast of current design trends, social media platform updates, and industry innovations. Incorporate fresh ideas and creative approaches into your content to stay relevant and attract attention.

- **Experimentation**: Don't be afraid to experiment with new creative formats, storytelling techniques, or visual styles. Encourage creativity within your team or collaborate with creative professionals to brainstorm innovative ideas.

6. Integrating Creatives with Monetization Strategies

- **Promotional Campaigns**: Use visually compelling creatives to promote products, services, or special offers. Highlight key selling points, discounts, or incentives to encourage conversions and sales.

- **Brand Partnerships**: Collaborate with brands to create sponsored content or co-branded creatives that resonate with both your audience and the brand's target demographic. Ensure that creatives align with brand guidelines and messaging.

- **Content Monetization**: Enhance the appeal of your content through high-quality creatives to attract more followers, increase engagement, and drive traffic to monetization channels such as affiliate links, paid subscriptions, or sponsored content.

Section Conclusion

Creating compelling content and mastering graphics are essential strategies for effectively monetizing your social media presence. By understanding your audience, setting clear goals, and implementing these tips and tricks for content creation and graphic design, you can attract and engage a loyal following, build credibility, and ultimately generate revenue through sponsored content, affiliate marketing, product sales, and other monetization avenues. Continuously refine your content strategy based on analytics and feedback to optimize performance and achieve sustainable success on social media.

Engage and Grow Your Audience

Growing a substantial and engaged audience is essential for making money on social media. A larger and more engaged following increases your influence, expands your reach, and opens up various monetization opportunities such as sponsored posts, affiliate marketing, selling products or services, and more. Here's a comprehensive guide on how to effectively grow an audience for monetizing your presence on social media:

1. Define Your Target Audience

- **Identify Niche**: Define your niche audience based on their interests, demographics, behaviors, and preferences. Understanding who your ideal audience is will help you tailor your content and engagement strategies effectively.

- **Market Research**: Conduct research to identify where your target audience spends their time online and which social media platforms they prefer. Use analytics tools and insights to gather data on audience demographics and interests.

2. Create Compelling and Valuable Content

- **Content Strategy**: Develop a consistent content strategy that aligns with your audience's interests and preferences. Create content that provides value, educates, entertains, or inspires your audience.

- **Quality Over Quantity**: Focus on producing high-quality content rather than overwhelming your audience with frequent but mediocre posts. Quality content tends to attract more engagement and shares, helping to grow your audience organically.

- **Content Variety**: Diversify your content by incorporating different formats such as videos, images, infographics, blog posts, live streams, and interactive polls or quizzes. Experiment with what resonates best with your audience.

3. Optimize Your Profiles and Posts

- **Profile Optimization**: Ensure your social media profiles are complete, professional, and aligned with your brand identity. Use a clear profile picture, compelling bio, and relevant keywords to improve discoverability.

- **Use Hashtags**: Utilize relevant hashtags in your posts to increase visibility and reach a broader audience interested in similar topics. Research trending and popular hashtags within your niche.

- **Engaging Captions**: Write engaging captions that encourage interaction and conversation. Pose questions, share personal stories, or include call-to-action (CTA) to prompt likes, comments, and shares.

4. Engage and Interact with Your Audience

- **Respond Promptly**: Actively engage with your audience by responding to comments, messages, and mentions promptly. Show appreciation for feedback and encourage two-way communication.

- **Initiate Conversations**: Start conversations with your audience through polls, Q&A sessions, or live streams. Encourage participation and make your audience feel valued and involved.

- **Community Building**: Foster a sense of community among your followers by creating discussions, featuring user-generated content, and acknowledging loyal supporters. Engaged communities are more likely to advocate for your brand and attract new followers.

5. Collaborate and Network

- **Influencer Collaborations**: Collaborate with other influencers, content creators, or brands within your niche. Cross-promote each other's content to reach new audiences and build credibility.

- **Participate in Groups and Communities**: Join relevant social media groups, forums, or communities where your target audience interacts. Contribute valuable insights, share your content, and network with members to expand your reach.

- **Attend and Host Events**: Participate in virtual or in-person events, webinars, or conferences related to your niche. Networking with industry professionals and thought leaders can help you gain exposure and attract followers interested in your expertise.

6. Promote Your Social Media Channels

- **Cross-Promotion**: Promote your social media profiles across different platforms, such as sharing your Instagram handle on Twitter or linking your YouTube channel in your Facebook bio. Encourage your audience to follow you on multiple channels.

- **Email Marketing**: Utilize your email list to promote your social media channels and encourage subscribers to engage with your content. Include social media buttons or links in your email campaigns to drive traffic to your profiles.

7. Utilize Paid Advertising

- **Targeted Ads**: Invest in targeted social media advertising campaigns to reach specific demographics, interests, or locations relevant to your audience. Use analytics to monitor ad performance and optimize targeting for better results.

- **Promoted Posts**: Boost your top-performing content through promoted posts to increase visibility and engagement. Experiment with different ad formats, placements, and budgets to maximize ROI.

8. Measure and Analyze Performance

- **Analytics Tools**: Use analytics tools provided by social media platforms (e.g., Instagram Insights, Facebook Analytics, YouTube Analytics) to track key metrics such as follower growth, engagement rates, reach, and conversions.

- **Performance Evaluation**: Analyze which types of content, posting times, and engagement tactics yield the best results. Adjust your strategy based on data-driven insights to optimize audience growth and content effectiveness.

9. Stay Consistent and Patient

- **Consistency**: Maintain a consistent posting schedule and engagement strategy to keep your audience engaged and attract new followers. Regularly review and refine your content strategy based on audience feedback and performance metrics.

- **Patience**: Building a sizable and engaged social media audience takes time and persistence. Stay patient and focused on delivering value to your audience, and growth will follow organically over time.

Section Conclusion

Growing an audience on social media requires a strategic approach focused on understanding your audience, creating valuable content, optimizing your profiles and posts, engaging with your audience authentically, collaborating with others, promoting your channels, utilizing paid advertising when appropriate, measuring performance, and staying consistent. By implementing these strategies effectively and adapting to audience feedback and platform changes, you can attract a loyal following, increase engagement, and unlock various monetization opportunities to make money with social media.

Explore Monetization Methods

Monetizing your presence on social media involves leveraging your audience and content to generate revenue through various channels. Whether you're an influencer, content creator, business, or entrepreneur, there are several effective monetization options available on social media platforms. Here's a detailed exploration of monetization options for making money with social media:

1. Advertising Revenue

- **Ad Placement**: Platforms like YouTube, Facebook, Instagram, and TikTok offer advertising revenue opportunities through ad placements in your content.

- **Ad Revenue Sharing**: Earn money based on the number of views, clicks, or impressions generated by ads displayed on your videos, posts, or stories. Revenue sharing models vary by platform and can include cost-per-click (CPC) or cost-per-thousand-impressions (CPM) rates.

2. Sponsored Content

- **Brand Collaborations**: Partner with brands to create sponsored posts, videos, or stories that promote their products or services. Brands pay influencers or content creators based on their reach, engagement rates, and target audience demographics.

- **Affiliate Marketing**: Promote products or services through affiliate links or unique discount codes provided by brands. Earn a commission on sales generated through your referral links or codes. Platforms like Instagram, YouTube, and blogs are popular for affiliate marketing.

3. Digital Products and Services

- **E-books and Courses**: Create and sell digital products such as e-books, online courses, workshops, or tutorials. Use platforms like Gumroad, Teachable, or your own website to host and sell your digital offerings.

- **Memberships and Subscriptions**: Offer premium content, exclusive access, or special perks through membership or subscription models. Platforms like Patreon or YouTube Channel Memberships allow fans to support creators through monthly subscriptions in exchange for exclusive content.

4. Direct Sales

- **E-commerce Integration**: Utilize social media platforms with integrated e-commerce features like

Facebook Shops, Instagram Shopping, or Pinterest
Buyable Pins to sell physical products directly to
your audience.

- **Dropshipping**: Partner with suppliers to sell
products without holding inventory. Use platforms
like Shopify integrated with social media to create
an online store and fulfill orders through third-party
suppliers.

5. Content Licensing

- **Sell Photography and Artwork**: Monetize your
creative work by licensing photos, artwork, or
designs for use in advertising, publications, or
merchandise. Platforms like Instagram or Behance
showcase your portfolio and connect you with
potential buyers.

6. Consulting and Services

- **Freelance Services**: Offer freelance services such
as graphic design, social media management,
content writing, or coaching based on your
expertise. Use your social media profiles to
showcase your skills and attract clients.

- **Coaching and Consulting**: Provide personalized
coaching, consulting, or mentorship services related
to your niche or industry. Use platforms like
LinkedIn or Twitter to establish thought leadership
and attract clients.

7. Live Streams and Virtual Events

- **Paid Live Streams**: Host paid live sessions, webinars, or virtual events where attendees pay for access to exclusive content, workshops, or interactive Q&A sessions. Platforms like YouTube, Instagram, or Twitch offer monetization options for live streaming.

8. Crowdfunding

- **Donation Platforms**: Use crowdfunding platforms like Patreon, Kickstarter, or GoFundMe to receive donations or pledges from supporters who appreciate your content or want to support your creative endeavors.

9. Selling Merchandise

- **Branded Merchandise**: Create and sell branded merchandise such as apparel, accessories, or merchandise featuring your logo, slogans, or artwork. Use platforms like Teespring, Spreadshirt, or Printful to handle production and shipping logistics.

10. Event Sponsorships and Partnerships

- **Event Sponsorships**: Partner with brands to sponsor events, contests, giveaways, or virtual meetups hosted on your social media platforms.

Brands benefit from exposure to your audience while you earn revenue from sponsorship deals.

Implementing Monetization Strategies

- **Choose Suitable Platforms**: Select social media platforms that align with your content, audience demographics, and monetization goals.

- **Build and Engage Your Audience**: Focus on growing a loyal and engaged audience through consistent content, interaction, and community building.

- **Diversify Revenue Streams**: Explore multiple monetization options to reduce dependency on one source of income and maximize revenue potential.

- **Comply with Regulations**: Adhere to advertising guidelines, disclose sponsored content transparently, and respect copyright laws when monetizing your social media presence.

Section Conclusion

Monetizing your social media presence involves leveraging your influence, content, and audience to generate revenue through various channels such as advertising revenue, sponsored content, digital products, direct sales, consulting services, live streams, crowdfunding, merchandise sales, and event sponsorships. By understanding your audience, choosing the right monetization strategies, and consistently delivering value through your content, you can effectively turn your social media presence into a profitable business or revenue stream. Continuously adapt and optimize your monetization efforts based on audience feedback, platform updates, and industry trends to achieve sustainable success on social media.

Learn and Adapt

Learning about your audience and adapting your strategies accordingly is crucial for effectively monetizing your presence on social media. Understanding who your audience is, what they want, and how they engage with your content allows you to tailor your approach, improve engagement, and optimize monetization efforts. Here's a comprehensive guide on how to learn and adapt to your audience for making money with social media:

1. Utilize Analytics Tools

- **Platform Insights**: Social media platforms like Instagram, Facebook, Twitter, and YouTube offer built-in analytics tools. Use these tools to gather data on your audience demographics, behavior, engagement metrics, and content performance.

- **Key Metrics**: Monitor key metrics such as follower growth rate, post reach, engagement rate (likes, comments, shares), click-through rates (CTRs), and conversion rates (if applicable). Analyze which types of content resonate most with your audience.

2. Audience Research and Segmentation

- **Demographics**: Understand the age, gender, location, language, and other demographic factors of your audience. Tailor your content and messaging to resonate with these characteristics.

- **Psychographics**: Explore the interests, preferences, lifestyles, values, and motivations of your audience. Conduct surveys, polls, or use social listening tools to gather insights into their interests and behaviors.

3. Engagement and Feedback

- **Two-way Communication**: Foster two-way communication with your audience by responding to comments, messages, and mentions promptly. Actively engage in conversations, ask for feedback, and encourage interaction.

- **Feedback Loops**: Use feedback from your audience to refine your content strategy. Pay attention to comments, direct messages, and social media polls to understand what content topics, formats, or styles resonate most.

4. Content Optimization

- **Content Analysis**: Evaluate the performance of your content regularly. Identify high-performing posts (based on engagement, reach, conversions) and analyze the factors contributing to their success.

- **Content Preferences**: Adapt your content based on audience preferences. Experiment with different formats (videos, images, infographics), tones (educational, entertaining), and themes to see what generates the most engagement.

5. Testing and Iteration

- **A/B Testing**: Experiment with different variations of content (e.g., headlines, visuals, CTAs) through A/B testing. Compare performance metrics to determine which version resonates best with your audience.

- **Iterative Approach**: Continuously refine your content and strategies based on performance data and audience feedback. Adapt to changes in audience preferences, platform algorithms, and industry trends.

6. Monitor Trends and Insights

- **Industry Trends**: Stay informed about trends and developments in your industry or niche. Monitor popular topics, hashtags, and emerging trends to create timely and relevant content that appeals to your audience.

- **Platform Updates**: Keep up-to-date with changes in social media algorithms, features, and policies. Adapt your strategy to leverage new features (e.g., Instagram Reels, Twitter Spaces) and optimize visibility.

7. Personalization and Segmentation

- **Segmented Content**: Segment your audience based on their interests or behavior. Create personalized content or offers tailored to specific segments to enhance relevance and engagement.

- **Dynamic Messaging**: Use dynamic content strategies to deliver personalized messages, recommendations, or promotions based on user interactions and preferences.

8. Collaborate and Partner with Your Audience

- **User-generated Content**: Encourage your audience to create and share content related to your brand or products. Feature user-generated content (UGC) to build community, showcase customer experiences, and foster authenticity.

- **Co-creation**: Involve your audience in content creation or product development processes through polls, surveys, or beta testing. Collaborate with them to create content that meets their needs and interests.

9. Adapt to Changing Audience Preferences

- **Flexible Strategy**: Maintain flexibility in your content strategy to adapt to evolving audience preferences and market dynamics. Be open to trying new formats, topics, or approaches based on audience feedback and performance metrics.

10. Measure Impact and Adjust

- **Performance Metrics**: Continuously monitor the impact of your adaptations on key performance indicators (KPIs) such as engagement, conversion rates, and revenue. Use data-driven insights to make informed decisions and optimizations.

- **Iterative Improvement**: Embrace a culture of continuous improvement. Test, learn, and iterate your strategies to optimize audience engagement, satisfaction, and ultimately, monetization outcomes.

Section Conclusion

Learning and adapting to your audience on social media involves leveraging analytics tools, conducting audience research, fostering engagement, optimizing content strategies, testing and iterating, monitoring trends, personalizing messaging, collaborating with your audience, and remaining flexible to changing preferences. By understanding your audience deeply, responding to their needs and interests, and continuously refining your approach based on data and feedback, you can maximize engagement, build loyalty, and effectively monetize your social media presence through various revenue streams. Adaptation and evolution are key to sustaining growth and success in the dynamic landscape of social media monetization.

Stay Compliant and Organized

Staying compliant when making money through social media is crucial to maintain trust with your audience, adhere to platform guidelines, and comply with legal regulations. Whether you're engaging in sponsored posts, affiliate marketing, selling products, or offering services, it's essential to understand and follow relevant rules and regulations. Here's a comprehensive guide on how to stay compliant for making money with social media:

1. Understand Advertising Guidelines

- **Platform Policies**: Familiarize yourself with the advertising policies and guidelines of each social media platform you use (e.g., Facebook, Instagram, Twitter, TikTok). Platforms have specific rules regarding sponsored content, disclosures, and promotional practices.

- **FTC Guidelines**: In the United States, the Federal Trade Commission (FTC) requires influencers and content creators to disclose paid partnerships, sponsorships, or endorsements clearly and conspicuously. Use hashtags like #ad, #sponsored, or #paid to disclose sponsored content.

- **ASA Guidelines (UK)**: If you're in the UK, adhere to guidelines set by the Advertising Standards Authority (ASA) regarding transparency in advertising and sponsorship disclosures.

2. Disclose Paid Partnerships and Sponsorships

- **Transparency**: Clearly disclose any paid partnerships, sponsorships, or promotional relationships with brands or advertisers in your social media posts. Disclosures should be upfront, unambiguous, and placed where they are easily noticed by your audience.

- **Disclosure Methods**: Use disclosure labels such as "Paid partnership with [Brand]", "Ad", "Sponsored", or similar terms at the beginning of your posts or in a prominent location (e.g., Instagram Stories disclosures).

3. Respect Copyright and Intellectual Property

- **Use of Images and Content**: Obtain proper licenses or permissions for images, videos, music, or any other content you use in your posts or advertisements. Avoid infringing on copyright laws and respect intellectual property rights.

- **Create Original Content**: Whenever possible, create original content or use royalty-free images and music to avoid legal issues related to copyright infringement.

4. Data Privacy and GDPR Compliance

- **General Data Protection Regulation (GDPR)**: If you operate within the European Union (EU) or handle data of EU citizens, comply with GDPR regulations regarding data privacy, consent, and data processing practices.

- **Data Handling**: Obtain explicit consent from users before collecting their personal data or using cookies for tracking purposes. Clearly communicate your data handling practices in your privacy policy.

5. Health and Safety Regulations

- **Product Claims**: If you promote or endorse products or services related to health, wellness, or safety, ensure that your claims are truthful, substantiated, and compliant with regulatory standards.

- **FDA Regulations**: In the United States, adhere to regulations set by the Food and Drug Administration (FDA) regarding the promotion of dietary supplements, drugs, cosmetics, and medical devices.

6. Tax Compliance and Financial Reporting

- **Income Reporting**: Report all income earned through social media monetization activities to tax authorities in accordance with local tax laws. Keep accurate records of earnings, expenses, and deductions related to your social media business.

- **Business Entity**: Consider establishing a legal business entity (e.g., sole proprietorship, LLC) for your social media monetization activities to manage taxes and liabilities effectively.

7. Avoid Deceptive Practices

- **False Advertising**: Avoid making false or misleading claims about products, services, or offers in your social media content. Ensure that your promotional messages are accurate, transparent, and aligned with reality.

- **Honest Reviews**: Provide honest and unbiased reviews of products or services. Disclose any material connections or incentives received from brands when reviewing or endorsing their products.

8. Stay Informed and Educated

- **Industry Updates**: Stay updated on changes in social media platform policies, advertising regulations, and legal requirements relevant to your monetization activities.

- **Professional Advice**: Consult with legal, tax, or compliance professionals if you have questions or concerns about staying compliant with regulations and guidelines.

9. Monitor and Respond to Changes

- **Platform Updates**: Regularly review updates to social media platform policies and guidelines.

Adapt your strategies and practices accordingly to maintain compliance with evolving standards.

- **Audience Feedback**: Pay attention to audience feedback, questions, or concerns related to your sponsored content disclosures or promotional practices. Address issues promptly and transparently.

10. Document Compliance Efforts

- **Record Keeping**: Maintain records of sponsored content agreements, disclosures, and communications with brands or advertisers. Document your efforts to comply with advertising regulations and legal requirements.

Section Conclusion

Staying compliant when making money with social media involves understanding and adhering to platform guidelines, FTC regulations on disclosure, copyright laws, data privacy regulations like GDPR, health and safety standards, tax compliance, avoiding deceptive practices, staying informed about industry updates, and documenting your compliance efforts. By prioritizing transparency, honesty, and legal compliance in your social media monetization activities, you can build trust with your audience, mitigate risks, and sustain long-term success in monetizing your social media presence effectively and responsibly.

Networking and Collaboration

Networking and collaboration are powerful strategies for expanding your reach, building credibility, and unlocking new opportunities to make money with social media. By connecting with like-minded individuals, influencers, brands, and businesses, you can leverage collective strengths, cross-promote content, and access new audiences. Here's a comprehensive guide on how to network and collaborate effectively for monetizing your social media presence:

1. Identify Potential Partners and Collaborators

- **Research and Identify**: Identify individuals, influencers, brands, or businesses within your niche or industry that align with your values, target audience, and objectives. Look for synergies and complementary strengths.

- **Social Media Platforms**: Use social media platforms, industry events, online communities, and networking tools (e.g., LinkedIn, Twitter chats, Facebook groups) to discover and connect with potential collaborators.

2. Build Genuine Relationships

- **Engagement**: Start building relationships by engaging with their content, sharing valuable insights, and showing genuine interest in their work.

Comment on their posts, share their content, and participate in discussions.

- **Direct Outreach**: Initiate direct outreach through personalized messages or emails to introduce yourself, express admiration for their work, and propose collaboration ideas that benefit both parties.

3. Collaboration Opportunities

- **Content Collaboration**: Collaborate on content creation such as co-authored blog posts, guest blogging, collaborative videos, podcasts, or social media takeovers. Combine your expertise and audiences to create valuable, engaging content.

- **Cross-Promotion**: Cross-promote each other's content, products, or services to reach new audiences and increase visibility. Share social media posts, tag each other, or mention collaborators in your content to drive traffic and engagement.

- **Joint Campaigns**: Partner on joint marketing campaigns, giveaways, contests, or challenges that incentivize audience participation and engagement. Pool resources, leverage collective reach, and amplify campaign impact.

4. Negotiate Terms and Agreements

- **Clear Expectations**: Define clear objectives, roles, responsibilities, and expectations for each collaborator. Discuss compensation, promotional strategies, content ownership, and timelines to ensure mutual understanding and alignment.

- **Contracts**: Consider drafting collaboration agreements or contracts outlining terms, deliverables, payment terms (if applicable), confidentiality clauses, and dispute resolution mechanisms to protect both parties.

5. Maximize Mutual Benefits

- **Value Exchange**: Focus on creating mutual benefits and value for both collaborators. Align your collaboration goals with shared interests, audience preferences, and strategic objectives to maximize impact and ROI.

- **Audience Alignment**: Ensure that your collaborator's audience aligns with your target demographic. Collaborate with partners whose audience demographics, interests, and purchasing behaviors complement your offerings.

6. Promote Authenticity and Transparency

- **Authenticity**: Maintain authenticity in your collaborations by aligning with partners whose values and brand ethos resonate with your own. Authentic partnerships build trust with your audience and enhance credibility.

- **Disclosure**: Transparently disclose any paid partnerships, sponsorships, or promotional relationships to comply with FTC guidelines and maintain trust with your audience. Use disclosure labels like #ad or #sponsored.

7. Evaluate and Measure Success

- **Performance Metrics**: Track key performance indicators (KPIs) such as engagement rates, follower growth, website traffic, sales conversions, or campaign reach. Analyze data to assess the effectiveness of collaborations and ROI.

- **Feedback**: Solicit feedback from collaborators and your audience to evaluate collaboration outcomes, identify areas for improvement, and refine future partnership strategies.

8. Expand Your Network Continuously

- **Networking Events**: Attend industry conferences, seminars, workshops, and networking events to meet potential collaborators, industry influencers, and thought leaders. Build relationships and explore collaboration opportunities offline and online.

- **Stay Active**: Stay active in online communities, forums, and social media groups related to your niche. Engage in discussions, share insights, and establish yourself as a valuable contributor to attract collaboration opportunities.

9. Long-term Partnerships and Relationships

- **Nurture Relationships**: Foster long-term relationships with collaborators through consistent communication, mutual support, and shared successes. Collaborate on multiple projects or campaigns to deepen partnerships and maximize ongoing benefits.

10. Adapt and Innovate

- **Adaptation**: Stay adaptable and open to exploring new collaboration formats, emerging platforms, or innovative partnership strategies. Experiment with different types of collaborations to discover what resonates best with your audience and achieves your goals.

Section Conclusion

Networking and collaboration are essential strategies for monetizing your social media presence effectively. By identifying potential partners, building genuine relationships, exploring collaboration opportunities, negotiating terms, maximizing mutual benefits, promoting authenticity, evaluating success, expanding your network, nurturing long-term partnerships, and staying adaptable, you can leverage collective strengths, expand your reach, and unlock new revenue streams through social media collaborations. Strategic partnerships not only enhance your content and engagement but also position you as a credible authority within your niche, driving sustainable growth and monetization opportunities on social media.

Stay Persistent and Patient

Staying patient and persistent is essential for anyone looking to make money through social media. Building a profitable presence on these platforms takes time, effort, and consistency. Here's a detailed guide on how to cultivate patience and persistence while striving for financial success on social media:

1. Understanding the Journey

- **Realistic Expectations**: Recognize that building a successful social media presence and monetizing it is a long-term endeavor. It typically doesn't happen overnight. Set realistic goals and milestones to measure progress.

- **Learning Curve**: Understand that there is a learning curve involved in mastering social media platforms, understanding your audience, creating engaging content, and implementing monetization strategies effectively.

2. Consistent Effort and Dedication

- **Content Consistency**: Consistently create and publish high-quality content that resonates with your audience. Establish a regular posting schedule and stick to it to maintain engagement and attract new followers.

- **Engagement**: Dedicate time to engage with your audience through comments, messages, and interactions. Building genuine connections and fostering a community around your content takes ongoing effort.

3. Building Trust and Credibility

- **Authenticity**: Prioritize authenticity in your interactions and content. Build trust with your audience by being transparent about your intentions, values, and the products or services you promote.

- **Quality Over Quantity**: Focus on producing valuable content rather than chasing follower counts or vanity metrics. Quality content builds credibility and encourages organic growth and audience loyalty.

4. Patience in Audience Growth

- **Organic Growth**: Understand that growing a loyal and engaged audience organically takes time. It involves consistently delivering value, understanding audience preferences, and adapting your strategies based on feedback.

- **Community Building**: Foster a sense of community among your followers by encouraging discussions, featuring user-generated content, and actively participating in relevant conversations within your niche.

5. Adapting to Changes

- **Platform Dynamics**: Social media platforms constantly evolve with algorithm changes, new features, and trends. Stay adaptable and be willing to adjust your strategies to leverage these changes effectively.

- **Market Trends**: Monitor industry trends, competitor strategies, and audience preferences. Adapt your content, monetization methods, and promotional strategies to align with current market demands and opportunities.

6. Managing Setbacks and Challenges

- **Resilience**: Expect setbacks and challenges along the way, such as fluctuations in engagement, algorithm changes affecting reach, or unsuccessful monetization attempts. Develop resilience to persevere through tough times.

- **Learning from Failures**: View failures as learning opportunities. Analyze what went wrong, gather insights from feedback, and use these lessons to refine your approach and improve future outcomes.

7. Seeking Support and Mentorship

- **Community Support**: Surround yourself with a supportive community of fellow creators, entrepreneurs, or mentors who understand the challenges of monetizing on social media. Share experiences, seek advice, and offer mutual encouragement.

- **Mentorship**: Consider seeking mentorship from experienced individuals who have successfully monetized their social media presence. Learn from their strategies, insights, and mistakes to accelerate your own growth.

8. Celebrating Milestones and Progress

- **Small Wins**: Acknowledge and celebrate small milestones and achievements along your journey. Whether it's reaching a follower milestone, achieving a high engagement rate on a post, or securing your first paid collaboration, recognize your progress.

- **Long-term Perspective**: Keep your long-term goals in mind while celebrating short-term successes. Each milestone signifies progress towards your ultimate objective of sustainable monetization and financial success.

9. Maintaining Balance and Well-being

- **Avoid Burnout**: Pace yourself and maintain a healthy balance between your social media efforts and personal well-being. Take breaks, practice self-care, and pursue hobbies or activities that recharge your creativity and motivation.

- **Mindfulness**: Practice mindfulness and stay focused on your goals without comparing your progress to others. Trust in your journey, stay committed to your strategies, and maintain a positive mindset during challenges.

10. Continuous Learning and Improvement

- **Educational Growth**: Stay curious and commit to continuous learning. Keep abreast of industry trends, attend webinars or workshops, and invest in courses or resources that enhance your skills in content creation, marketing, and monetization.

- **Iterative Approach**: Embrace an iterative approach to improvement. Continuously analyze data, gather feedback, experiment with new strategies, and refine your tactics to optimize performance and maximize monetization opportunities.

Section Conclusion

Successfully making money with social media requires patience, persistence, and a long-term commitment to building an engaged audience, creating valuable content, and implementing effective monetization strategies. By maintaining realistic expectations, consistently delivering quality content, adapting to changes, managing setbacks, seeking support, celebrating milestones, prioritizing well-being, and continuously learning and improving, you can navigate the challenges of social media monetization with resilience and determination. Stay focused on your goals, trust in the process, and remain persistent in your pursuit of financial success on social media.

THE WRAP UP

In the realm of social media marketing, building authentic relationships with your audience is paramount. It goes beyond mere transactions; it's about fostering genuine connections that resonate and endure.

The foundation of these relationships lies in authenticity. Your audience craves transparency and sincerity. By sharing your brand's values, mission, and stories in an honest and relatable manner, you establish trust and credibility.

Consistency is equally crucial. Regular interaction and engagement demonstrate your commitment to listening and responding to your audience. Whether through responding to comments, sharing user-generated content, or initiating conversations, consistency reinforces your presence and reinforces the bond with your community.

Empathy plays a pivotal role in nurturing relationships. Understanding your audience's needs, challenges, and aspirations allows you to tailor your content and messaging to resonate on a deeper level. By showing empathy and addressing their concerns, you demonstrate that you value their feedback and prioritize their satisfaction.

Strategic storytelling becomes the vehicle through which these relationships are forged and strengthened. By crafting narratives that evoke emotion, inspire action, or provide value, you create a connection that transcends the digital realm. Authenticity in storytelling humanizes your brand, making it more relatable and memorable to your audience.

Analytics serve as your guide in this journey. They provide insights into what resonates with your audience, helping you refine your strategies to better serve their needs and preferences. By leveraging data intelligently, you can tailor your approach to maximize engagement and foster deeper connections.

Ultimately, success in social media marketing hinges on the quality of relationships you build with your audience. It's about moving beyond metrics and transactions to cultivate a community that believes in your brand, advocates for your values, and feels valued in return. By prioritizing authenticity, consistency, empathy, and strategic storytelling, you pave the way for meaningful and enduring relationships that drive sustained growth and loyalty in the digital age.

About the Author:

Rich Packer is a seasoned marketing professional with over a decade of combined experience in graphic communications and digital marketing. His journey through these dynamic fields has equipped him with a multifaceted skill set that spans creative design, strategic marketing, and cutting-edge digital tactics.

In the realm of digital marketing, Rich has honed his expertise in leveraging various platforms and technologies to drive impactful campaigns. His proficiency in social media marketing extends beyond mere engagement metrics, focusing on cultivating meaningful interactions that foster brand loyalty and advocacy. Rich understands the nuances of crafting compelling content tailored to different social channels, ensuring maximum reach and engagement.

With a keen eye on SEO (Search Engine Optimization), Rich has mastered the art of optimizing content to enhance visibility and organic search rankings. His strategies are grounded in data-driven insights and a deep understanding of search engine algorithms, enabling him to achieve measurable results for his clients.

Rich is also a forward-thinker in marketing trends, staying ahead of industry shifts and emerging technologies. He continuously evaluates new tools and methodologies to innovate marketing strategies that resonate in an ever-evolving digital landscape. His proactive approach to staying abreast of trends ensures that his work remains at the forefront of industry standards.

Through his writing, Rich aims to share his knowledge and passion for effective digital marketing practices. He is committed to empowering professionals to navigate the complexities of modern marketing with confidence and creativity. Rich's dedication to bridging the gap between design aesthetics and marketing strategy underscores his commitment to driving success for brands in today's competitive market environment.

Rich holds a firm belief in the transformative power of strategic marketing and continues to push the boundaries of what's possible in digital communication and brand storytelling.